Making the Deal

Making the Deal

Quick Tips for Successful Negotiating

George M. Hartman

John Wiley & Sons, Inc.

New York ■ Chichester ■ Brisbane
■ Toronto ■ Singapore

This publication is designed to provide accurate and authoritative information in regard to the subject matter covered. It is sold with the understanding that the publisher is not engaged in rendering legal, financial, or other professional services. If legal advice or other expert assistance is required, the services of a competent professional person should be sought.

Library of Congress Cataloging-in-Publication Data

Hartman, George M.
   Making the deal : quick tips for successful negotiating / by
George M. Hartman : illustrations by Bill Kobe.
      p.   cm.
   Includes bibliographical references.
   ISBN 0-471-54378-0. -- ISBN 0-471-54379-9 (pbk.)
   I. Negotiation in business. I. Title.
HD58.6.H38   1992
S58.4--dc20   91-41086
                                                 CIP

ISBN 0-471-54378-0 Cloth
     0-471-54379-9 Paper
Printed in the United States of America
10 9 8 7 6 5 4 3 2 1

Printed and bound by Malloy Lithographing, Inc.

"The old idea of a good bargain was a transaction in which one man got the better of another. The new idea of a good contract is a transaction which is good for both parties to it.**"**

Justice Louis D. Brandeis

CONTENTS

ACKNOWLEDGMENTS

One evening, while on a business trip, I had some time to kill, so I toyed with some ideas about creating a book that would present the militia of tips and techniques I'd accumulated on closing deals or reaching agreements more quickly. (Like many other business travelers, I strove to get a meeting finished even before it began.) I thought of the tactics I had often created on the spot when traditional tactics had failed to consummate a negotiation. My book would differ from other books on the same subject by including unorthodox negotiation tactics used by experienced negotiators to supplement the regularly prescribed strategies and tactics. Furthermore, I would show how to relieve the frustration of an impasse by adding a touch of humor to what is often labeled an "impossible situation." And I would treat the opposing party (often referred to as an opponent) as an ally rather that an adversary. (When I first began negotiating, I, indeed, did regard the opposing party as an adversary. With experience, I learned that better results were obtained by treating an opponent as a friend.)

Consequently, my list of acknowledgments must begin by thanking my former manager at Unisys, Charles Villota, who sent me out of town without much experience and threw me into the world of negotiation and let me sink or swim. Fortunately, I knew how to swim!

I also want to thank the National Contract Management Association, which instills interest and knowledge of negotiation by way of seminars, symposia, and workshops. With this assistance, I was able to include consideration of both buyers and sellers.

My remaining acknowledgments are certainly numerous but for the sake of brevity will be limited to those individuals who are particularly worthy of mention:

- First, my wife, Audrey, who patiently listened to some of the cornier stories and whose editing and grammatical input were of foremost importance

- Second, those who contributed anecdotes about tactics experienced during negotiations

- Third, those knowledgeable authors whose books with related material about the strategies and tactics of negotiations were inspirational

- Finally, my close friend, Dr. Roberta Levitt, who, as an excellent educator, collaborated in the creation of the self-evaluation quiz in Chapter 1

PART I

Negotiating and You

_____

CHAPTER **I**

Introducing Negotiations and Negotiating

Have you ever analyzed why you didn't make that sale, didn't get that raise, or gave in on a deal too soon? Did the other party make you feel somehow inferior or create the illusion that you were a loser?

Whether we realize it or not, we are negotiating every day—with our spouses, our children, our friends, our local merchants, in our occupations, as sales representatives, and, foremost, in conducting business. Answers to the questions above may therefore be obvious—we all can use some knowledge about negotiating that will help us feel like winners. But to accommodate everyone's needs is an overambitious endeavor for an author whose experience has been primarily in contract negotiations. Consequently, this book is confined to those whose occupations require using negotiating skills to complete business deals. It is intended to serve both the novice and the experienced; whether the business is commercial or government-oriented, the principles and techniques of negotiation are equally applicable. That is, in every negotiation, the participants consist of two opposing sides—a buyer and a seller (or a salesperson).

An adequate description of negotiation means different things to different people:

- To the buyer, negotiation is the art of buying fine French champagne with a beer-budget pocketbook, and

- To the seller, negotiation is the art of selling a Mercedes to a buyer who pretends to be able to afford only a Hyundai.

However, one definition of negotiation that applies to any situation, business or otherwise, is:

The process of communication by which two parties, each with their own viewpoints and objectives, attempt to reach a mutually satisfactory agreement on a matter of common concern.

The objective of negotiating that is shared by both parties is to reach a fair and reasonable agreement that satisfies each party. For example, in the buyer/seller relationship, the seller expects to make a reasonable profit besides receiving reimbursement for all costs associated with producing goods or services, whereas the buyer strives to obtain the lowest price for goods or services of the highest possible quality.

Successful negotiations should result in win-win agreements that are in the best interests of both parties. Neither party should feel like a total winner or a total loser. Obtaining win-win agreements requires:

- Thorough preparation

- Clear presentations and evaluations of both sides' positions

- Skill, experience, motivation, and open-mindedness

- A reasonable approach for establishing and maintaining sound, cooperative, and mutually respectful relationships

- Willingness to make concessions to reach an agreement by compromise when an impasse occurs

Negotiating can be compared to bidding at a bridge game. Someone must open the bidding, and the responses must continue until agreement is reached, that is, when the bidding stops. Bridge requires skill in evaluating the cards that one is holding, knowing what strategy to employ in bidding, and deciding which cards to play. Also, in playing bridge, like negotiating, *you've got to give to get!*

Similarly, negotiation should continue until an agreement between the parties is reached. To avoid a rupture in the process, experienced negotiators save face by applying tactics that fall into the category of gamesmanship. These tactics are often used to save what seems to be a lost cause. Sometimes, introducing humor at a crucial time when nothing else seems to work can resolve an impasse and reach an agreement that previously seemed impossible. Thus, the potential cost of negotiation, in terms of both time and expense, can be kept reasonable and within allowable administrative budgets.

On the other hand, a negotiator must know when to stop negotiating. There's a breaking point in every negotiation. If you push too far, your opponent may react irrationally and walk out. *Remember: To label negotiations successful, both sides should feel as if they've won.* After all, the relationship between both parties usually continues beyond reaching an agreement. If the parties are bound by contract, their association may continue until the contract is completed. Or they may be jointly involved in other business opportunities in the future.

This book has been organized into three parts:

1. Part One includes an overview to introduce negotiating techniques and to define those traits and skills that make a good negotiator.

2. Part Two explores negotiating skills, including strategies and tactics, preparing for meetings, reaching agreements through compromise, and applying gamesmanship.

3. Part Three provides information about projecting a proper appearance and image, conveying proper body language, and ethical behavior during negotiations. This section also includes information on how to select the negotiating team, evaluate proposals, and recognize personality traits to help understand and deal with difficult negotiators and also discusses similarities between negotiators and sales representatives.

The art of negotiation requires skills and knowledge gained more from experience than from formal education. An experienced negotiator who has had formal training in the negotiation process and in applying negotiating strategies and tactics can be recognized as a leader who takes the initiative, maintains control, and is a good motivator. Although other books have been previously published on negotiating strategies and techniques, few of them have addressed the expeditious handling of negotiations or how to face the challenge negotiating presents.

To achieve quicker agreements through negotiations, the negotiator can employ three primary techniques:

1. Developing a **strategy** prior to conducting negotiations, or during the earlier stages of a negotiation session

2. Using **tactics** or textbook methods at any time during negotiation to assist in reaching agreement

3. Creating non-standard tactics, or **gamesmanship**

With knowledge of those techniques, you're on your way to acquiring negotiating skills that you can use for the rest of your life.

CHAPTER 2

An Overview of Negotiation Skills

Good negotiating skills not only make you a winner but also make your opponent feel like a winner. The results should always appear as if both sides end up in a satisfactory win-win situation. After all, you probably will have to deal with him or her again sometime in the future, for additional business deals or for assuring satisfactory completion of delivered goods or services.

To obtain or improve your negotiating skills, you can participate in more and more negotiation sessions, attend educational workshops, assist in the development of plans and in the preparation for negotiations, practice the techniques of negotiating, and evaluate results. Experience and active participation are the key factors.

As you become an experienced negotiator, you will learn to:

- Evaluate the efficacy of negotiations during and after completion of a negotiation session, and

- Outline actions to improve the quality of future agreements

Good negotiating skills should include being an excellent communicator, observing and reading people, and the ability to think on your feet. The quality of communication skills can be measured by how well your side and the opposing party's side comprehend your presentation, counteroffers, and, finally, the discussions that lead to an agreement. Be aware of the surrounding activity, observe personality traits of members of the opposing party; listen carefully to hear what is being said, not just what is being told to you. In negotiating, in particular, when responding to demands, you want to know the path the opposing party is following. The more you know about your opponent, the more effective you will be. With these skills, you can obtain vital information by learning what your opponent really wants, enabling you to reach agreements quicker. Often, by being alert, you recognize hidden conflicts that may be the cause of a deadlock.

A win-win situation requires skilled negotiators to determine both areas of agreement and disagreement and how to amicably reconcile differences. Activities that allow for mutual trust to be developed between both parties will make any negotiation more efficient and rewarding. You may reach agreement more quickly by reviewing each party's objectives, proposing solutions to resolve disagreements, and minimizing any differences.

What Makes a Good Negotiator

What makes you a good negotiator?

Of all the possible combinations of personality traits, skill, motivation, self-confidence, and power form a desirable network to influence a negotiator's personality. With these traits, or the development of improved traits, you should get the results you want—more often and more quickly—and minimize the expense of negotiations. Experience, education, and practice leads to developing and establishing yourself as a good negotiator. Measurement of the degree of how good you are depends on how well you have adapted yourself to negotiating.

Skill encompasses knowledge of negotiation techniques, strategies, and tactics. (These techniques will be discussed in later chapters.)

Motivation influences the outcome of negotiations. A negotiator who is highly motivated will have a strong desire to demonstrate why his or her demands should be accepted by the other party. This trait requires good communication skills in order to make demands understood. The negotiator will rely on spontaneous feedback to measure how well he or she is proceeding so that on-the-spot adjustments to any demands can be made.

Self-Confidence is developed by the negotiator's maturation and experience. If you fear failure, you may lack confidence. In order to combat your fears, you must change your attitude and improve your negotiating skills. Confidence will come with experience. The more you learn, the more successful you will be.

Power is often necessary for achieving agreements. If you are able to recognize that an opponent is trying to control negotiations, you will have an edge and be able to respond in an equally authoritative (though not overbearing) manner. A very persuasive opponent who displays aggressiveness usually has a great need to win arguments. But if either party is overpowering or monopolizes the exchange of information, reaching an agreement may be impossible. On

the other hand, one must be flexible and willing to yield some-
what, even if it means compromising.

Besides being skillful, motivated, self-confident, and powerful,
a negotiator should be able to:

- *Plan:* Experienced negotiators believe that the most
  productive time in the negotiation process is spent in
  planning. A negotiator should be able to separate con-
  tested issues and develop a salable position that can
  produce a successful agreement before sitting down at
  the negotiating table. The ability to plan may be acquired through business education and experience.

- *Behave with integrity:* A negotiator's integrity or ethical
  behavior is extremely important. An organization's
  image is directly affected by the integrity of its key
  representatives, including its negotiating team. Individuals who act without high integrity and behave
  unethically can destroy the image of an organization.
  (Ethical behavior is covered more fully in Appendix
  A.)

- *Think clearly while under stress:* During negotiations,
  while the negotiator is under pressure to perform, it's
  crucial to think clearly on the spot so that you can
  develop good arguments. Learn to relax prior and during meetings by recognizing that conflicts go with job
  responsibilities.

- *Use good judgment:* Sound decisions (rebuttals or counteroffers) are based on carefully assessing the other
  party's presentation and responding appropriately. Development of good judgment is primarily based on
  experience—opportunities to observe others in action
  and learn from your own mistakes.

■ *Listen:* Successful negotiators listen carefully to all discussions. As they listen, they test the validity of what is being said to assure that it is meaningful. Good negotiators are prepared to alter their positions when logical arguments are presented by opponents. It takes discipline and concentration to develop good listening habits.

■ *Be emphatic:* Empathy means having sensitivity for the feelings of others so that a satisfactory rapport with the opposition can be established.

■ *Communication:* A negotiator must communicate well both verbally and in writing. Here again, education and experience are the keys to developing this ability. The more you participate, the more you improve your skills.

Test Your Negotiating IQ
True or False

_____ 1. Prior to the negotiation session, it is best to learn as much as possible about the subject matter and about your opponent.

_____ 2. Team members who talk out of turn can disturb the negotiations and possibly give you an advantage.

_____ 3. The negotiator should be recognized as the team manager.

_____ 4. Schedule negotiation sessions as close to your deadline as possible.

_____ 5. Make your opposing negotiator feel comfortable.

_____ 6. Always follow your opponent's agenda for the meeting.

_____ 7. Good negotiators are active listeners.

_____ 8. An opening offer should be based on an estimate of a reasonable range of probable costs.

_____ 9. The negotiation process requires that both parties aim toward achieving a settlement.

_____ 10. Never assume that your opening demands are high enough or low enough.

_____ 11. Never make a concession without getting one in return.

_____ 12. Avoid questions that are either controversial or ambiguous.

_____ 13. A negotiator should have the ability to plan.

_____ 14. Cost only is extrapolated from technical descriptions of proposals.

_____ 15. A proposal should be reviewed initially to identify any information or clarifications needed.

_____ 16. A negotiator should perform a risk appraisal as part of design, schedule, and cost proposal evaluations.

_____ 17. A negotiator can always negotiate without a team effort.

_____ 18. If your opponent shouts, you should respond by shouting louder.

_____ 19. Good judgment comes from experience and from opportunities to observe others and learn from past mistakes.

_____ 20. No skills are necessary to be an effective questioner.

Answers

1. T		11. T ✓	
2. F		12. T	
3. T		13. T	
4. F		14. F ✓	
5. T		15. T	
6. F		16. T	
7. T		17. F	
8. T		18. F	
9. T		19. T	
10. F ✓		20. F	

After you have checked your answers, circle those you answered incorrectly. Incorrect answers can be a road map to indicate areas of weakness, so you may want to turn to the area of this book that covers those skills that need refinement.

PART II

Negotiating

Skills

CHAPTER 3

Preparation: The Key to Successful Negotiations

Before meeting with the opposing party, you should try to learn as much as possible about him or her. Research your opponent, consider the other company's performance history, review other deals your opponent has closed (or even better, couldn't close) and why. If possible, get to know your opponent before the negotiation session begins, perhaps with an informal get-together during a coffee break or over lunch.

There are a number of additional items to keep in mind prior to the start of a negotiation. These items, as highlighted and summarized in the next two paragraphs, are concerned with adequate preparation.

Establish an opening position and a target agreement. Never enter a negotiation without having a bottom line. You should be able to walk into a conference confident that you will conclude with a satisfactory deal. (Protect yourself from accepting a bad deal on an impulse to rush the negotiation.) The more willing you are to risk losing a deal, the more power you show. When negotiating a product or service, the seller's proposal should be evaluated in advance of the negotiation.

Sort out the potentially difficult issues and prepare alternative solutions. *Creativity is the key to a successful negotiation.* Put yourself in your opponent's shoes by recognizing that he or she has multiple interests, many—if not most—of which may parallel yours. Don't prematurely judge what those interests are or search for a single simple answer. It may be worth some effort to spend time determining how your opponent will react to your presentation. Solving your opponent's problem may be like solving your own.

Fact-Finding

Sometimes it is beneficial to hold a fact-finding session that precedes the negotiation session for the purpose of extracting information. Fact-finding may be considered as the initial step toward reaching agreement. The fact-finding session is attended by both parties' negotiators and designated negotiating team members. Questions are prepared in advance of the meeting and presented in clear, concise language without being ambiguous or controversial and without putting the other party on the defensive. Both parties must attempt to be cooperative by being fully responsive.

Questions or discussions at the fact-finding session may concern specific items, such as:

- Acquiring more information about your opponent's proposal

- Explanations of derivations of methodology in providing numbers for labor, material, rates, etc.

- Resolving unsatisfactory answers

- Specific details of the proposal

- Reviewing points of disagreement (usually, this item
  is saved for last)

Assessing Your Opponent's Position

Schedule a fact-finding meeting with your opponent prior to
the negotiation session, as discussed earlier. Spend this time
determining areas of agreement and disagreement, separating
minor issues from major issues. Subsequently, the negotiations
can focus on collaborative problem-solving with utmost effi-
ciency.

Knowing your opponent is an important part of assessing his
or her position. People are usually predictable. If she did it
before, she's likely to repeat herself. What strategies did she
previously use? What can other people tell you about her?
Has she written anything that provides clues? Consider her
constituency—who does she report to? Who are the real decision makers, if not her immediate supervisor? How can you
help her to deal with her constituency?

Research the background of her firm prior to entering negotiations by reviewing the firm's history, its policies, and its
financial condition. Also determine whether the firm is cur-
rently involved in any litigation that could interfere with making a legitimate agreement. (More about getting to know your
opponent is covered in Chapter 10.)

Developing the Perfect Plan

If a proposal has been submitted before a negotiation begins, start by evaluating its contents. With or without a proposal, rehearse your negotiation plans. When will you present your position? What information will you use in support of your position? What is your opponent's likely response, and what will your response be in defending your position? Fully explore the alternatives and options available to you in the event that you don't reach a timely agreement (considered in Chapter 4). Outline these alternatives in order of preference, and be ready to present them to avoid a breakdown in negotiations.

Choosing and Managing Your Negotiating Team

The need for team support for proposal preparation/review or negotiation depends on the complexity of the program of the impending contract to be negotiated. The advantages of having a team must be weighed against disadvantages.

The advantages:

- Teams are frequently more creative than individual negotiators. Team members' different technical backgrounds can provide a wealth of knowledge and information.

- It is best to have assistance when covering complex, high-priced programs that make negotiations difficult.

- If your opponent is bringing in a team, it is advisable to do the same to avoid an imbalance of attendees at the negotiation table.

The disadvantages of having a team may be more compelling in some circumstances. The negotiator must evaluate each situation as it is presented. Some of the considerations that militate against having a team are:

- The fewer participants, the quicker an agreement may be achieved.

- Team members who talk out of turn can disturb the negotiations and possibly give your opponent an edge.

- Differences of opinion among team members can weaken your side's position. It is most embarrassing to have team members argue among themselves at the negotiating table.

When selecting a team, never include members who are not needed. Use only members with excellent credentials who will be most constructive and supportive.

CHAPTER 4

How to Open Negotiations

Assuming the negotiation requires a team effort, some precautions should be taken prior to the start of the negotiation session. If a member of the negotiating team is detrimental or disruptive in reaching an agreement, either exclude the person or ask him or her to leave the negotiation. Use acknowledged experts with greater credibility and who are constructive, personable, and more influential. Technical personnel should be available for consultation but excluded from the team unless their presence is necessary because of program details. Also, beware of the team member with the need to talk!

As the designated negotiator, you should be recognized as the team manager. It is your responsibility to:

- Try to keep the numbers of team members on each side even.

- Make sure that everyone on your team understands what is and is not ethical.

- Arrange a method of signaling among team members (someone may have thought of something not previously discussed, which may require calling a caucus).

- Emphasize the need for security or privacy, which may limit access to information discussed during negotiations.

- Assign individual responsibilities (by technical ability) for replying to questions (this will help avoid having your opponent take advantage of weaker team members).

- Make sure that everyone on your team understands the limitations of his or her authority.

(More about negotiating team members is covered in Chapter 9.)

The Right Time

When establishing dates for negotiating with the opposing party, it is to your advantage to schedule negotiation sessions as close to your opponent's deadline as possible. Most concessions that lead to agreement occur immediately before a deadline.

Midweek days are better days to negotiate. From my own experience, I have found that Mondays are often sluggish after a weekend off, and negotiations are rushed on Fridays because no one wants to work over weekends. I recall many times when I have had to rush to catch a plane at a New York airport for an early morning flight to Los Angeles so that a meeting could begin on a Monday afternoon. I learned the hard way that this gave my opponent an edge.

The Right Place

Usually it's best to hold negotiation sessions in your own territory. You can gain a psychological edge when your opponent comes to you; your resources are readily available, your eating and sleeping schedules are not disrupted, and you may attend to regular business routines.

But even if the session is scheduled at your opponent's facility, you still have certain advantages. You get the opportunity to see your opponent's operations firsthand. You can devote your full time and attention to negotiations, while your opponent may be interrupted by other duties; you can plead lack of authority or information; and, if necessary, you can ask your opponent's supervisor for assistance. Both, pleading lack of authority or information and asking the opponent's supervisor for assistance, are tactics that may be used to your advantage and readily employed when at your opponent's facility.

From my experience, I prefer to meet at my opponents' facilities because I can thereby avoid interruptions by business associates and phone calls. Also, access to my opponents information and their staffs provides the necessary backup material to assist in reaching quicker agreements. My opponents also prefer meeting at their own facilities for reasons that were previously given above.

However, getting to a meeting that is remote is both time-consuming and expensive (for airfare, hotel room, meals, and lost time in travel). Besides, you may be distracted or frustrated by menial things, like getting a good night's sleep (especially when there's a change in time zone) or finding the facility or the meeting place. Also, your regular work load may be disrupted, which may cause missed deadlines for other programs.

So, where should the negotiation session take place? The answer may require reviewing advantages and disadvantages in accordance to the estimated dollar value of the program before drawing any conclusion. A buyer is more influential in making the decision. For convenience of both parties, a neutral site can be selected—a meeting place halfway between your facility and your opponent's facility. Or, both negotiating teams can stay at home base and negotiate via a communications satellite and by the latest available technology—the visual telecommunications conference screen. This screen is especially useful for fact-finding meetings, but it may be perceived as too impersonal for negotiations.

Seating and Other Physical Arrangements

Negotiating team members tend to sit at the opposite sides of a conference table, and their team leaders normally at opposite ends of the table. Human engineering studies have shown that individuals who vie for the upper hand seek out a true "power seat," one that faces away from a window and towards a door.

To avoid creating animosity, some alternative seating arrangements may be worth trying. Sitting at a round table tends to improve cooperation and encourages both parties to feel as if they are jointly facing a task. Sitting side-by-side, or at right angles, tends to create feelings of closeness and collaboration between people. But there may be some disadvantage in these arrangements; your opponent may have the opportunity to read your notes if he or she is blessed with the ability to read upside down. Thus, a compromise seating arrangement may be best, such as sitting diagonally across the table as shown in Figure 1. Also, to help you remember names of attendees, it is suggested that you make a seating chart using team members' names around the table (also shown in Figure 1). Your team members should be seated near you so that they are readily accessible for consultation.

Attendees: Pass an attendance sheet around in a clockwise direction and begin with:

Judith   Alexandra
John   Maxine
Your Opponent George
Alan   Yourself

Figure 1: Negotiation Session Seating Arrangement

The negotiating environment is critical. In selecting a meeting room, consider:

- Lighting—Bright but soft illumination is preferable.

- Room color—A beige or pastel color is less distracting than bright colors.

- Room size.

- Availability of a telephone—The telephone should be located to provide privacy.

- Noise level—A meeting room within an administration area is better than one near the factory.

- Air conditioning—The room's temperature should be set by its own thermostat.

- Refreshments—As a minimum, provide coffee and hot water for tea and decaf, but don't go overboard in serving bakery goods.

- Nearby caucus rooms.

- Availability of computers and calculators—Small desktop units are preferred.

- Chair types—Comfortable chairs are a must, especially for meetings of long duration.

- Audiovisual equipment, if required.

- Copying and fax facilities.

- Administrative assistance—Secretarial and clerical types should be available.

Be a good host by making your opponent and his or her team members as comfortable as possible. Make the negotiation session as convenient for your opponents as you would want in return. Tell them where to find rest rooms, the cafeteria or nearby restaurants, and so on.

Establishing a Positive and Relaxed Atmosphere

Spend some time showing some personal interest in your opponent. Introduce your team members. Be casual, friendly, and relaxed. Review the rules of the negotiation; you should stress that you will be most satisfied with a win-win outcome. You should also say that you are prepared to consider all reasonable alternatives and that you do not believe in playing any tricks or games (that is, you want to proceed on an ethical basis).

Learn the names of everyone on the other side, and use their first names often; refer to your seating chart.

At the outset, try to take control of the session. Suggest breaks and make lunch arrangements, initiate the discussion at the end of the get acquainted period, and propose an agenda.

Don't enter a negotiation session with a chip on your shoulder. Resolve to remain cool and courteous under all circumstances. Get the negotiation moving by agreeing on minor issues. Save the tougher ones for later, after a climate of trust and respect has been developed.

Setting an Agenda

An agenda controls what will and will not be discussed and the sequence of the discussion. Always prepare your own negotiating agenda, but first get your opponent's agenda. You need not follow your opponent's proposed agenda unless it suits your purposes, but you should review and study his or her agenda before negotiating because it may reveal important strategies, positions, and assumptions. Beware of what your opponent may have left out; this omission may be intentional.

Discuss your key issues as close to the end of the negotiation session as possible. Start off with easy-to-settle issues. If you or your opponent's key issues come up earlier than you had planned, defer their discussion until the easier issues are settled. Do not risk an early confrontation.

Formulating an Opening Offer/ Position

Negotiations normally involve a sequence of offers and counteroffers. At the start of this sequence, the party that is soliciting an agreement is first to make an offer. His or her opponent will then reply with a counteroffer. This process will continue back and forth like a tennis match until both sides feel that they have reached an amicable agreement.

To illustrate how to formulate an opening position, let's refer to the buyer/seller relationship. The seller would have submitted an opening offer with his or her proposal. The buyer must prepare a counteroffer. However, if the buyer suspects that the seller's proposal no longer fully meets the intent of the original solicitation, based on new information or discussions with the negotiating team members during the proposal evaluation stage or at fact-finding meetings, the seller may be requested to resubmit the proposal prior to the negotiation session.

Dealing with Conflicts

Conflict is a part of life that must be endured. Recognize that negotiations may involve a tug-of-war between the two parties. As a negotiator, you may spend a substantial amount of time saying things your opponent does not like and does not want to hear; therefore, you must expect negative reactions.

Negotiating is stressful, and the stress increases as discussions approach agreements or before making concessions. It is vital to separate personalities from the problem (refer to Chapter 11 for details about negotiators' personalities). When the conflict extends beyond the propositions represented by the negotiators and starts to involve the personalities of the negotiators themselves, it is serious. To avoid a misunderstanding, point out the advantages of your proposal instead of the problems of your opponent's position. Under no circumstances should you try to cause your opponent to lose face.

Communicating Effectively

Try to have your opponent express a position before you express yours. To show your attentiveness, summarize your opponent's position frequently. It is gratifying to all of us to know that we have been heard and that our positions are understood. Lead-ins like "Let me see if I've understood what you're saying" or "So what you're saying is . . ." may be used.

Being belligerent and argumentative wins you nothing. Whenever possible, use questions, which are much less threatening, than emphatic statements.

Improving Your Listening Skills

Good negotiators are active listeners. Do not stop listening because you are thinking about what you will say next. Instead, jot down notes and refer to them when you are given the opportunity to reply. Even if it becomes tempting to stop listening because you think you know what your opponent is going to say, remember that this assumption may prove embarrassing if you guess wrong.

Many companies offer their employees courses in the listening techniques. Audiocassettes are also available that encourage developing good listening skills.

You can improve the effectiveness of a negotiating session by actively listening to what your opponent is saying. Remember, you have two ears and one mouth; therefore, listen to what is being said twice as often as you talk! By demonstrating patience and a genuine interest in what is being said, each party can help the other reach a quick and painless agreement. By listening, the chance of misunderstanding is minimized. Consequently, you help yourself achieve a satisfactory win-win agreement more expeditiously—your objective from the start of negotiations.

Your opponent wants and needs your approval; you can show it by listening. Don't interrupt. Let your opponent ramble. If you don't understand, let your opponent know and be specific about the items that you have difficulty understanding.

Follow some of the techniques created by sales representatives when closing a sale. Do not be afraid to ask dumb questions. If you are having difficulty formulating a question, ask for help; your opponent will volunteer to get you out of the hole. But never use questions to show how clever you are or ask questions that can create animosity or start fights. Attribute aggressive questions to absent third parties: "My purchasing manager asked me whether your price is realistic."

Prepare and occasionally ask "test" questions to which you already have answers. Have many of your questions ready in advance of the negotiation. Ask your question, then shut up!

If you open your mouth first, you may let your opponent off the hook.

Words of Caution

- Take care of all personal needs prior to the meeting, to avoid unnecessary interruptions.

- Ask that everyone refrain from smoking or limit the smoking by creating smoking and nonsmoking sections at the negotiating table.

- Use a secretary or appoint a scribe to record items that may be emphasized during discussions and prior to making a final offer or reaching an agreement.

Getting to that Agreement Quicker

In this and the previous chapter, we have been dealing with preparatory activities prior to the negotiation session, all of which are necessary to enhance effective negotiating and minimize the duration of the negotiation. For example, the buyer in preparing his or her offer would have done homework by reviewing the seller's proposal against budget limitations, estimating costs, and comparing the proposal to the estimated costs. Furthermore, the buyer may have also planned options to reduce costs and to bring the costs within budgetary limitations.

The preparation of options can be the key to making negotiations run smoother and to break deadlocks (refer to Chapter 8). Options may be used to modify or postpone work or program tasks, alleviate schedules and delivery requirements. In some extreme cases, the type of contract (e.g., fixed price vs. time and material reimbursement) and incentives for profit (e.g., for improved performance for quality or earlier deliveries) may be suggested to ease problems in reaching agreements.

CHAPTER 5

Strategies and Tactics: Differentiating the Techniques

Strategy is defined in Webster's Unabridged Dictionary as "a careful plan or method or a clever stratagem," whereas *tactics* refers to any method used to gain an end—in our case, reaching an agreement in making the deal.

Both strategy and tactics require having special skills in adapting procedures or techniques to negotiation applications. Successful negotiations do not begin at the negotiation table; they result from careful planning and detailed preparation. Negotiations involve opposing parties—a *buyer*, who seeks specific products or services from a qualified source whose price and supporting data are acceptable, and a *seller*, who convincingly presents a rationale for why his or her proposal should be accepted.

Strategies vs. Tactics Employed in Negotiations

Strategies include a variety of plans and premeditated techniques. They should help you conduct sessions amicably so that you conclude with an agreement that is satisfactory to both sides. Experienced negotiators use a variety of means to accomplish their objectives. Knowing when to use a particular strategy properly involves a sense of timing and skill in application that should lead to a successful conclusion without either party considering itself a loser.

Using tactics skillfully, however, means applying more spontaneous methods for seeking an agreement when strategies fail. Although I've attempted to distinguish them, in practice, strategies and tactics are often interchangeable.

Whether employing either strategies or tactics, it is important that the negotiator behave ethically. An atmosphere of respect between the negotiating parties should be maintained at all times. Normally, each party should act responsibly by avoiding surprises and by cooperatively exchanging current, accurate, and complete data and information.

Planning which questions to ask during negotiations is part of preparing for the negotiation. (The same types of questions apply to the fact-finding meeting that precedes the negotiation as well.) Questions should be designed so that they obtain information that has been concealed. Questions fit into the following categories:

- *Direct*: A direct question is very specific. For example, you may ask your opponent to provide a rationale for a specific item under review. "Why are you marketing this widget at eighty-five cents each?" But, always wait for your opponent's answer. If the answer is unclear, redirect your question or repeat your opponent's answer as you understand it. "At eighty-five cents, we would only net two-and-a-half cents per unit. Is there a reason you are keeping the price so low?" The process may be iterative until a satisfactory answer is obtained.

- *Factual*: A factual question asks for information about actual data. For example, "What are the sales to date of the first widget you sold this year?"

- *Leading*: A leading question attempts to get affirmative answers. For example, "We would be able to begin distributing the widget by this fall, right?"

- *Delegated*: A delegated question addresses questions to someone else on your opponent's negotiating team. This may force the other side's negotiator to reply to the question which you believe he would have avoided if asked directly. For example, ask a specialist to explain the importance of his or her efforts as they contribute to the success of the program. "Margaret, how do you feel the special sales department will handle the widget? Can you sell it to your contacts?"

At both negotiation sessions and fact-finding sessions, avoid asking questions that are either controversial or ambiguous. However, sometimes these types can be used intentionally to camouflage real issues that if approached directly may bring only veiled answers.

It takes skill to ask questions that can elicit appropriate answers. Effective questioning usually is developed through experience in negotiating. Exchanging questions and answers is part of the process of negotiating. To be an effective questioner, the negotiator should be on the lookout for ambiguous or inane (versus intelligent and meaningful) answers. Your opponent may intentionally provide responses that lead you to a hasty agreement that you may regret later.

Like negotiating, effective questioning does not follow scientific rules but is more of an art. Questions are selected according to the type of negotiation. For example, sales representatives learn to ask questions that require affirmative responses. When trying a case, lawyers seem to have the knack of asking witnesses the "right" questions to get the answers that will support their arguments. Like negotiators, lawyers prepare themselves with appropriate strategies. Many questions are delivered spontaneously at negotiations, but as previously noted, they are usually provided to your opponent in advance of a fact-finding meeting to allow for adequate preparation on his or her part.

Remember that effective questioning should be approached in a manner that does not cause embarrassment. State your questions explicitly. Do not assume your opponent knows your organization's lingo or acronyms; he or she may be reluctant to answer or may be afraid of being embarrassed by showing ignorance. On the other hand, if your opponent uses words or asks questions that you do not understand, do not reply until you have requested and received clarification. Also, avoid using:

- All-inclusive or overly general terms (e.g., all, about, and everybody)

- Ambiguous phrasing that lessens the chance of getting a straight answer

- Loaded or slanted questions that force prejudicial answers

- Leading questions that may result in improper answers

Questions can also be grouped according to what kind of answer the questioner desires: open-ended or free response questions, two-way questions, and multiple-choice questions. Open-ended questions allow the person being queried to give opinions rather than absolute answers, for example, "Do you think this widget would be better sold in stores or via mail order?" Two-way questions enhance communication and cooperation of both sides for exchanging thoughts and ideas, for example, "I think I know the answer to why you have selected that method to fabricate this widget, but could you verify my explanation?" Multiple-choice questions enhance replies for clarifying positions, for example, "What color should the widget be: red, white, or blue?"

Examples of Negotiation Strategies

Introducing combinations: One party introduces a combination of several negotiable items at the start of the negotiation session. In this way, concessions can be made for some items within the combination, and gains may be possible for others when accepting a combination. Some of the negotiable items may be considered "throwaways"—that is, one party may have had every intention of conceding them to the other party some time during negotiations. However, *nothing should ever be conceded without making certain the other party knows that it is getting a concession.* Concessions can then be emphasized later in the negotiation as a reminder and used as a bargaining (or trading) point.

To illustrate: A proposal contains a detailed breakdown of labor to be used in support of an impending program. To review each category separately would be tedious. Instead, you combine labor into one or more groups (e.g., shop and engineering) and counteroffer with less labor hours.

Using broad coverage: One party may attempt to do a broad-brush treatment and avoid reviewing details. In this way, minor issues or areas can be covered without expending excessive effort and time in the negotiation session.

To illustrate: One party may want to negotiate a contract on a total cost basis instead of tediously reviewing one cost element at a time. However, the other party may oppose this by insisting that each cost element be considered separately so that the pricing details of the proposal will get appropriate and adequate attention. (Possibly, the first party may prefer negotiating on a total cost basis to avoid discussing individual cost elements that, if altered in any way, may either force a major repricing effort or changes on its part.) To compromise, parties may agree to skip over cost elements of low values.

Moving one step at a time: This is an effective strategy whereby one minor point after another is convincingly presented until the initiating party has won a major concession. However, each concession must be addressed separately to see how it fits into the overall picture.

To illustrate: The negotiation begins by reviewing a lower-cost part of a proposal—the page count for supplying instruction and maintenance manuals for a certain product—rather than first reviewing the labor or material cost elements for producing the product. A concession is reached; a cost figure is established based on actual figures from a previously complete program that had been negotiated between the two parties. By starting with minor issues the big items may be easier to handle later.

Using statistics: "Figures don't lie, but. . . ." Each party to the negotiation must make certain that any figures and statistics (e.g., inflationary trends, material costs) that are presented are valid and reliable. This is another case in which adequate preparation pays off.

To illustrate: One party may argue that certain statistical trends are representative of the total cost proposal. The opposing party should be prepared to either refute or agree to the assertion. For example, labor statistics may be checked through the use of the Bureau of Labor reference material which provides actuals and trends in labor costs per locale. Data for materials often are readily available from computer files that contain actual purchases and quotations.

Examples of Negotiation Tactics

Showing patience: This approach involves delaying, suspending, or putting off an answer at the moment, thereby giving your team a chance to think over the opponent's proposition. On the other hand, the opponent also has the same opportunity to delay and may react by retracting its offer after further consideration. Another possibility is that the opponent may be elated that its proposal is getting serious consideration. But in the event a proposal is withdrawn, time should not be wasted discussing it. Unfortunately, showing patience is a time killer and delays reaching agreement.

In my experience, I have rarely found showing patience to be advantageous. In fact, I found it was detrimental because my opponents were given fresh opportunities to readdress their proposal and rework their cost estimates, which resulted in higher revised cost proposals. But if the differential in price between the original proposal and its revised version were measured against the cost of additional administrative tasks spent in extending the negotiation, many times the differences offset one another.

Using surprise: This tactic involves a sudden shift in one party's position or approach, which may catch the opponent off guard.

To illustrate: One party decides, without warning, to replace the team's engineer as the technical discussion leader. This may permit a new approach in reviewing and restating a major point to emphasize its importance. The opponent can look upon this tactic favorably and feels that there will be a better chance of reaching agreement, especially if it perceives the replacement as being more cooperative than the predecessor.

Employing diversion: In this situation, one party acts as if it has more information than it really does possess. This tactic may be considered as a bluff; thus care must be taken so as not to make unfounded claims or to be accused of unethical behavior, for example, overstating future needs or production quantities in anticipation that the other party will then reduce the price.

Manipulating participation: One party attempts to reduce the participation of opposing negotiating team members. This tactic is perhaps most common to negotiations that deal with complex programs or products.

To illustrate: If a deadlock appears inevitable for a particular item under discussion, one party may suggest that a splinter meeting be held with one comparably ranking member from each team until an agreement is reached by this group and brought back to the negotiation session.

Blaming a third party: To avoid admitting your own mistakes or faults, accuse someone else in your firm's organization of not providing you with adequate backup or information.

To illustrate: You gloss over weaknesses of your side's position to buy time for reworking a counteroffer with your management. (Often a manager is rightfully blamed for not commenting on preparatory material that had been submitted for his or her review.) Or, the engineering representative on your team may require additional time to organize his thoughts before continuing the negotiation.

Applying pressure tactics: Consider warning the other party in some fashion that the negotiation might have to be concluded prematurely if the other side does not budge on an issue. Resolve differences, but avoid a "take it or leave it" attitude. Issuing ultimatums will most likely sting you every time; you may be labeled as being noncooperative.

To illustrate: Your patience is waning, issues have been discussed repeatedly, and you've reached a point of exhaustion. Your deadline for reaching agreement is nearing. It may be time for gamesmanship (refer to Chapter 8)!

In opposition, prolonging the negotiation tests a negotiator's patience and may force concessions from the opponent. Here again, like the *showing patience* tactic, this may unnecessarily prolong the negotiation and be counterproductive. Experience shows that both parties dislike delays and are usually eager to reach an agreement most expeditiously.

When one party recognizes an opponent's tactics, a negotiator may change tactics that he or she feels will productively accomplish reaching agreement. Here's where experience pays off!

CHAPTER 6

Finding a Compromise

Compromise often produces agreements. The negotiation process requires both parties to aim toward achieving a settlement. If a final agreement is to be reached, a compromise may be the only means of accomplishing it in some situations. When compromising, the negotiators first summarize each other's relative positions, then point out specific areas of differences, and finally present facts or judgmental opinions in support of their own positions.

Types of **Compromise** may be defined where:

- each side establishes its "last" position prior to being willing to compromise

- compromise is considered the last step in negotiations

- both sides may have some feeling of satisfaction (e.g., having reached an agreement with the "best" price being acceptable to both parties)

- experienced negotiators reach compromises; but if one side is stronger than the other, a compromise may be imbalanced. It may satisfy one side but *not* the other!

CHAPTER 7

What Went Wrong? How to Avoid Tactical Mistakes

In gaining experience as a negotiator, you often learn by experiencing your mistakes. To help minimize mistakes and help you to negotiate successfully, consider the following tactical mistakes that should be avoided:

Making unreasonable opening demands: Never assume that your opening demands are too high (for a seller) or too low (for a buyer). By aiming at extremes, you give yourself room to negotiate. On the other hand, your opening demands should not be so unrealistic that your opponent decides not to bother with you and walks away from the negotiation.

To illustrate: You, the buyer, have done your homework and determined an estimated price range that will provide room for compromise. And you have dealt with your opponent, the seller, in past negotiations. From your experience, your going-in position would ordinarily be the lowest figure, but this may aggravate the seller. What should you do? Prior to the negotiation, you could review past negotiations that previously took place with the seller to determine how first offers compared with final price agreements. You might then determine a new first offer by using a percentile difference to a predicted final price.

Making free concessions: Never give a concession without getting one in return. Each concession should be emphatically conditioned so that the opponent understands that you are requesting one in return: "If you'll do this, I'll do that!" Unconditioned concessions frequently turn into freebies because your opponent will not reciprocate unless forced to.

To illustrate: As a seller, you are ready to concede to reducing the price of an item that had been delaying the agreement, but how can you give in without losing face? You could agree on that particular item but request an increase in a previously agreed-to price for a different item.

Starting without a shopping list: Do not bargain until you get your opponent's demands (or shopping list). Ask your opponent to place all demands on the table, but try to conceal yours until afterwards.

To illustrate: In preparing for the negotiation, you and your team establish what would be considered acceptable for the opponent's delivery performance. You keep this information in your back pocket until you listen to what your opponent has to offer. If both parties are attuned to each other's demands, many of your demands may be met without your having to negotiate for them.

Negotiating too rapidly: Making deals too quickly induces greater risk. Rapid settlements are frequently extreme win-lose deals. The less prepared and the less skilled negotiator is often victimized by an opponent. Put yourself in command; slow things down.

To illustrate: When one is a neophyte in negotiating, the tendency is to avoid the embarrassment of revealing weakness by reaching a quick agreement, and to wish the meeting was over before it starts. The neophyte may end up feeling like a loser upon rehashing the events afterwards. For example, a less skilled negotiator may yield to the opponent if he or she is not powerful enough to continue rationalizing a counter-demand.

Overcoming the urge to settle too quickly: Get into the habit of really reflecting on your opponent's position and mulling over the advantages and disadvantages of acceding to his or her demands, particularly if you have any questions or doubts about any matter. Resist pressures for a rapid decision. As illustrated above (in *Negotiating too rapidly*), satisfactory win-win deals are almost never bargained too quickly! (Most concessions occur near a deadline.)

Negotiating when surprised: Do not bargain over an issue unless you are fully prepared! When something unforeseen comes up, take a break. Call for a caucus with your team to review the new idea. Give yourself time to think about it.

To illustrate: You prepared for the negotiation by reviewing a proposal submitted by your opponent, but at the negotiation session, your opponent presents new facts (e.g., changes in product design, or schedules) based on studies conducted after the proposal was submitted. Don't lose your cool. Instead, request additional time for preparation of the negotiation. However, before caucusing, make certain you and your team understand the significance of the new data.

Honoring unreasonable demands: Never respond to an unreasonable demand with a counteroffer; instead, insist that your opponent reduce his or her demand! If he or she refuses, respond with an equally extreme counteroffer. Any other response may give your opponent something for nothing. But avoid any confrontation that may cause postponement of the negotiation.

To illustrate: Your opponent demands that senior personnel staff the program. You recognize that this is a ploy to squeeze out more money, so you counteroffer with use of junior personnel.

Being afraid of silence: By keeping your mouth shut, you can put your opponent under tremendous psychological pressure. After you have asked a question or while you are in the process of thinking, keep quiet. Do not be embarrassed about long silences during the negotiation session.

To illustrate: Your opponent makes an unfounded statement and adds a contingency factor to its bottom line price. You are dumbfounded by this addition, so why not ask for reasons to back up this factor? Ask and attentively listen to the answer. Do not interrupt your opponent, but wait until the explanation is completed. Hold any further questions until afterwards.

Getting angry: Keeping your cool gives you a great advantage over your opponent. Never lose your temper in a negotiation— or at least try not to show it. The person who is too emotional may not think clearly under pressure.

To illustrate: You get so irritated by your opponent's unreasonableness that you forget your prepared strategy and react too hastily to what the other side says. Instead, resist your natural tendency to respond! If you get angry, caucus or take a break. If you are still angry afterwards, have yourself replaced as the negotiator because you may no longer be effective.

Not getting it in writing: It is not enough just to reach an agreement. You need to get it in writing. A handshake is fine as long as things are working out, but finish with a written document that incorporates the major points of the deal and get it signed by both parties. This document may also serve as the outline for a formal contract. (See Chapter 9 for a sample Memorandum of Agreement.)

Negotiating when fatigued: Tired negotiators often make foolish errors. They are easily influenced by their opponents. Marathon sessions and late-night deals should be avoided. Be sure to get a good night's sleep prior to any negotiation session.

To illustrate: After spending the better part of a day traveling and rushing to be on time to a meeting, you feel exhausted. If you scheduled the meeting for the next day, wouldn't it be less stressful?

Letting your guard down: A few moments of carelessness can squander the results of a long, successful negotiation. Your opponent may have been waiting for a chance to take advantage of you. This is especially true when it's time to sign the agreement. Regardless of who prepared the agreement, check the fine print, line by line.

To illustrate: As Yogi Berra said, "It ain't over 'til it's over!" In negotiations, you should not relax until after you have a bona fide written agreement that is entirely concurrent with a verbal agreement.

DWI (Dealing While Intoxicated): Be aware of a common tactic that may be used by the opposing team's negotiator when inviting you to lunch at a restaurant that has a cocktail hour offering two-for-the-price-of-one cocktails. *Do not be tempted!* This may be an innocent gesture but is more likely an intentional tactic. Be suspicious and do not let your guard down or be naively persuaded! Instead of ordering liquor, order a soft drink such as club soda or ginger ale. After negotiations are completed and an agreement has been reached, you might suggest that your opponent joins you for a celebratory cocktail.

The message here is *Don't Drink While Negotiating* if you want to keep your wits about you. Remain in control to reach a satisfactory agreement instead of one that you may later regret.

Knowing when to stop negotiating: There is a breaking point in every negotiation. If you push too far, you may cause your opponent to react irrationally and walk out. *Remember:* A successful negotiation makes both parties feel like winners.

CHAPTER **8**

Gamesmanship

What happens when you run out of gas? You've diligently applied all your negotiation strategies and tactics, but instead of the negotiation proceeding amicably it has puttered and has come to a halt, and your opponent has become your adversary. Suppose for example, that you cannot convince your opponent to settle by splitting the difference between both final offers; do you hide under the table because you feel ashamed, or do you stand up like David challenging Goliath?

To assist you in reaching the agreement you want, this chapter covers gamesmanship tactics, which are often used by experienced negotiators under extreme or adverse conditions.

Gamesmanship, most often, is extemporaneous. It may be a last-ditch effort that is created by a negotiator, or an unconventional tactic that forces the other side to come to its senses and reach an agreement that had been avoided all along.

Note that often, when dealing with the same opponents over and over again, other negotiators learn to predict your moves. Thus, gamesmanship, as used by experienced negotiators, provides less likelihood of recognizable or predictable tactics. It avoids giving the other side an edge in negotiations by being able to predict your moves.

Breaking Deadlocks

A deadlock is often mistaken as a failure. It is frustrating and creates clashes of personalities between the negotiators. You may blame yourself for failing to reach an agreement and search for an answer as to what went wrong. And your opponent may be equally uncomfortable. As much as it is disliked, a negotiator should never be afraid to call a session deadlocked and suspend negotiations. This tactic gives everyone the opportunity to cool off and resume negotiations later, under calmer circumstances.

A deadlock on one or more elements of a negotiation does not mean that the entire negotiations is stalled. The knottiest issues can be set aside while other issues that are easier to resolve are negotiated.

Some additional tactics for breaking deadlocks include:

■ Changing the members of your negotiating team

> *To illustrate:* An engineer who has a delegated responsibility to assure that staffing of a program is reasonable refuses to listen to her opponent's explanations and insists that she is right. The negotiator decides to caucus with his team to determine why the engineer refuses to budge. It is discovered that the engineer has a grudge against the opponent. To resolve this deadlock, the engineer must be replaced.

■ Changing the impending program's work content, schedules, or separately priced items into smaller work packages

To illustrate: Break down the program into smaller, less complex items, and review and reach agreement on an item-for-item basis. For example, instead of negotiating the program based on a fully-assembled product (e.g., an electric motor), base it on major subassemblies or components (e.g., rotor, stator, and bearings).

■ Altering terms and conditions, payment arrangements, type of contract or introducing options

To illustrate: The buyer's terms and conditions require delivery at the buyer's facility. But the seller prefers acceptance at his plant and responsibility for delivery (that includes both transportation and insurance charges) by the buyer. Since the latter method may add insurance costs that the buyer will have to assume but will minimize the cost for requiring the buyer's quality control inspectors attendance at the seller's plant instead of performing the inspection at the buyer's facility, the cost trade-off is insignificant. But, to break the deadlock, the buyer agrees to the change.

■ Calling in a new negotiator or changing the negotiation team, asking to have your opponent's superior present, or turning over the negotiations to your superior. Understandably, neither negotiator is satisfied with applying any of these three tactics. He or she normally won't take the initiative but may be directed or forced to follow one or more of these tactics.

To illustrate: The negotiator spokesperson for the buyer could not make up his mind and kept vacillating in deciding to accept the seller's final offer, whose price exceeded his budget. To break the deadlock, his superior, the director of procurement, was asked to intercede. After reviewing the situation by hearing both sides, she took on the responsibility by accepting the final offer.

- Inventing one of your own unique tactics, following the examples in the next section.

More Creative Solutions

Sometimes humor can rescue a situation that seems insurmountable. A joke or lighthearted comment that brings laughter or smiles can break the tensions of negotiating. Those who can inject humor at the right time and use it wisely are more likely to sidestep the frustrations of failure. Rather than bemoan mistakes, laughing at ourselves or at our circumstances may overcome a conflict, meet the challenge, and succeed in obtaining that elusive agreement.

A good sense of humor usually indicates a positive state of mind. As an emotional expression, humor has a salutary effect upon both mind and body. However, laughter should appear sincere and spontaneous. The use of profanity is not necessary in getting your points across. Substitute a mildly self-deprecating joke instead that may give you an air of humility.

Many of the anecdotes that follow are not textbook cases of negotiations, but they illustrate tactics used to salvage tough negotiations. Some may be very down-to-earth, while others exemplify how a negotiator can be original and creative and adapt to difficult situations. I hope these anecdotes will offer some suggestions to help you originate a tactic or introduce a skill that you can use to reach that elusive agreement.

Role Playing

Role playing can be performed prior to a second round of negotiations. Its purpose is to prepare your team—after experiencing a day's worth of give-and-take with your opponent—to respond to what you predict will be your opponent's next strategies. In the previous day's events, you may have become aware of the types of strategies and tactics they were using. Here's how role playing works:

Select the person whom you consider your most cooperative and talented team member and let that person play the devil's advocate by representing the opposing negotiator. Go through the motions of an entire negotiation procedure, from the initial meeting of both sides through reaching an agreement, reviewing key points and counterpoints with all your team members present. Play-act your caucuses, primary arguments, offers, and counteroffers. With your objectives in mind, play out the strategy that you think your opponent will use.

If the negotiation is away from your home base, the most suitable time to perform this rehearsal is after dinner in a comfortable area of the hotel when everyone is relaxed. But keep the meeting short, no more than two hours. If the negotiation is at your facility, delay the next negotiation session for a few hours. Take advantage of being at your own facility by selecting a peer from your department who is heavily experienced in negotiating, instead of a team member, to play the devil's advocate. His or her fresh approach, without having attended the first session may be advantageous by not being influenced by previous discussions.

Confession

Sympathy can be used to get the other party to be more receptive to your position, especially for establishing a bottom-line price agreement. Therefore, why not try a tactic—making a confession—that has a fairly good track record.

When everything else fails, spill the beans and confess that your bottom-line dollar figure is all that you have been authorized to commit. Any demand for additional money would result in breaking off the negotiations, requiring you to return to your home office to consult with your manager and get your manager involved (up to now, you had been on your own and fully responsible for the outcome). Then shift into "good-guy bad-guy" mode. "Since my manager is a tougher negotiator than I, you've got more to lose by causing further delays in reaching an agreement. He's tough, he'll see to it that you'll squirm, and you'll probably end up with the short stick. So let's wrap this up here and now by accepting my last offer!"

Emotional Rescue

Never let your emotions—or your opponent's emotions—interfere with negotiations. For example, your opponent may begin to talk loudly, make accusations, or behave aggressively. He or she may sigh with disgust, slam papers down, or otherwise act in ways that provoke an emotional response from you. Listen carefully and don't interrupt! When the outburst is over, thank your opponent for expressing his or her position so emphatically. Keep cool, do not lose control, and speak softly. When your opponent speaks loudly, you should respond in a low (and soft-spoken) voice. Some negotiators may try to upset you by injecting emotion-laden statements into the negotiations, interrupting your thoughts and disrupting your planned strategies. Look squarely at your opponent if he or she is trying to be manipulative. Make it very clear that if your opponent doesn't get off your back, the negotiations may have to be delayed or canceled altogether. But be ready to resume after your opponent calms down and discusses details in an appropriate manner.

Feedback

Many times you must be alert and listen to your opponent for clues to what tactics you may select in getting that agreement; this is feedback.

While striving to reach an agreement on a price for a program that required retrofitting equipment in the field, the opposing negotiator was being assisted by a project engineer who was doing all the talking. Up to that point, agreement was obtained on manufacturing hours, but there was no agreement on the proposed engineering hours. The engineer refused to provide adequate backup for data on the engineering hours and claimed they could not be reduced. However, she had to excuse herself at quitting time to catch her car pool. And I was nearing the time I had to depart, since the next day I was scheduled to begin a management training course at home base.

So, here we were deadlocked on the engineering hours with only the two negotiators left to wrap it up. As I questioned her further, my opponent explained how superior her pricing estimators were in providing estimated labor hours. "In fact," she said, "from past experience, their estimates were always within 10 percent of actuals!"

Bingo! I found the key that I was looking for. I made her a counteroffer by accepting the accuracy of her estimators and presented her with figures that represented a 10 percent reduction for both manufacturing and engineering labor hours. At that point, she realized what she had said. In order to save face, she recommended that we split the difference. Since the bottom-line price was within my price objective, we reached agreement.

Help

If during negotiations an issue arises that catches you by surprise and you are unprepared to review it, stop the session immediately. You may wish to bring in some help from one of your experts. This maneuver can be used to buy time to think. Call for a caucus, take a coffee break, visit the restroom, or break for lunch (with your team members only). Buy time to discuss the specifics with either your team or with a phone call to your home office to speak to the expert, if necessary.

Just In Time

A good tactic to remember when negotiating is that both parties, even though they are reluctant to show it, are eager to reach an agreement. That is why most negotiations are concluded near the end of a session—just in time for the visiting team to catch its scheduled flight. Thus, the advice here is: Don't fret or lose your cool if the time is fleeting and an agreement is not in sight. Last-minute manipulations may make it possible to either reach an agreement on time or, if necessary, pick up where you leave off by scheduling another session. (Obviously, it is less desirable to continue at another time because of the expense of reconvening or causing a delay in starting a program.)

The Napkin Close

We were in the third day of a knock-down, drag-out negotiation, and we had not reached an agreement. I decided to make one last-ditch effort before terminating the session. I called for a caucus and asked my team members if we could make any further concessions, to which they replied that we were already at the upper price limit that we had established prior to the negotiation. Any further change would require a complete reevaluation and analysis, and resubmittal to our management for approval. But my feeling at this time, as it always has been during any negotiation, was to avoid returning home defeated.

Hence, I decided to do something different to break the deadlock. I took a napkin from a coffee table and wrote our final offer—a total price—between the folds. After calling the other team back into the room, I handed my opponent the napkin. He took one look at it, opened it, grinned, wrote something on it, then handed it back to me. I was delighted and surprised to read his "OK" adjacent to my offer.

The Phone Call

If there is difficulty in reaching an agreement, take the opponent's last offer (however unreasonable it may seem) and ask where you may make a phone call in privacy to your manager at your home base so that you may get concurrence or approval. Of course, you know full well what your limitations are (i.e., last position or final counteroffer).

Get on the phone (make sure your call is completed), but instead of your manager, call your spouse, your bookie, your sibling, or anyone who may answer the phone! Talk sufficiently long enough to be convincing. Then, take your time before returning.

Come back with a sob story, "My manager is unhappy! However, in order to avoid jeopardizing the excellent cooperation we've had between our firms that has been established over the years, and in order to continue that way in any future endeavor, she advised me to reach an amicable agreement. Thus, we're willing to meet you halfway," etc., etc.

Zorro

Sometimes, one member of the negotiating team likes to demonstrate power by attacking a member of his or her own team or a member of the opponent's team (usually one who holds an equivalent position). Often, a person who is being attacked will retaliate and become equally hostile. As the designated negotiator, what can you do about this escalating situation?

If the person who acts like Zorro (sword in hand and ready for a duel) happens to be on your team, interrupt the meeting and calm the person down. Then speak to the person privately, requesting that he or she remain cool so that the negotiations may continue with proper rapport.

If Zorro is a member of the opponent's team, interrupt the meeting and request that the other team's negotiator step outside. Politely recommend that the other team's negotiator handle Zorro by using the same tact as you would apply to a person on your team.

If both sides have Zorros, let them duel! But after allowing sufficient time to elapse, blow your whistle and, with the cooperation of the other team's negotiator, get the negotiation back on course by applying both of the previous suggestions or by using other techniques (e.g., caucus, ask the Zorros to meet separately or leave).

PART III

The

Professional

Negotiator

CHAPTER 9

The Elements of Style

It is worthwhile to cultivate the personality traits of the successful negotiator and to develop complementary skills that will smooth the road to desirable agreements. In addition, however, there are four issues that can decidedly alter the effectiveness of negotiations:

- Your appearance and behavior during negotiation

- The composition of the negotiating team

- The memorandum of agreement

- Terms and conditions

Appearance and behavior—body language—can reveal much of a person's mood, intent, and character. The subtlety of facial and hand movements discloses much about our opponent and ourselves. But body language can be controlled to some degree, and our opponent's signal can be evaluated for truth or deception. Picking the right players for the negotiating team is crucial for success. And, the memorandum of agreement is one of the most important documents that will have to be drafted during the negotiating process.

Your Appearance

Take a look at yourself in a full-length mirror. How do you appear to your colleagues and to your opponent? What kind of an impression do you give? Try to evaluate your appearance—are your projecting a negative image (for example, through a clenched jaw or bad posture) or a positive one? The negotiator with a confident stance, whose appearance enhances his or her presentation, is more likely to close more deals quickly.

You are on display during negotiations, and your first impression may be everlasting. Do you ever wonder how well you connect with people and understand their needs, respect their positions, and recognize their strengths and shortcomings? If you are aware of your own assets and limitations, you can often assess others' assets and limitations and reach a harmonious relationship.

Aside from your personality, your physical appearance is of utmost importance. Your dress and deportment reflect your authority, credibility, and appeal.

Are you aware of what kind of signals you project when you speak and respond to others? Are you also aware of your opponent's body language? You may be sensitive to body language, but so may your opponent! Therefore, you must be cautious of making any gestures that may give your position away. The primary and foremost signals are made by the eyes. Eyes can show anxiety or anger or reveal friendship, trust, and approval. For example, staring can indicate hostility and disrespect.

Facial gestures can also reveal one's feelings or thoughts, but the same gesture may be ambiguous. A smile can show either friendliness or animosity; one must be sincere when smiling to avoid being thought of as sarcastic. Dry lips often show fear and tension, so keep you lips moist. Coughing can project nervousness, so keep a handkerchief or a glass of water close by.

Using eyeglasses as a prop in projecting one's thoughts is common. Observe the glasses-in-mouth gesture—it frequently occurs at the end of negotiations when a decision is required. Also, peering over the glasses makes the opponent uneasy.

Be aware of hand signals—do you have clenched or open fists? Clenched fists may show anger and hostility, whereas open fists reveal friendliness. Handshakes reflect one's level of security. A firm handshake indicates confidence, but the bonecrusher may project insecurity, and the wet and clammy handshake, nervousness.

Arm gestures, such as folding the arms across the chest, send a strong signal that indicates that a person feels threatened. One arm folded in front of the chest with the hand clutching the other arm is an attempt to disguise nervousness. Leg positions can also project signals—crossed legs can indicate tension while stretched legs can connote a relaxed attitude.

Beware, however, of relying too heavily on body language for reading your opponent's mind. For example, an indication of good communication is eye-to-eye contact, but there are several ways of interpreting gazes. Furthermore, expressions that Americans customarily use may have different meanings in others' cultures and could prove embarrassing to both parties if misinterpreted. For example, when greeting people from a distance, we may raise our eyebrows, repetitively or for short durations. But in Japan, this gesture is considered indecent. Furthermore, in many cultures people express approval by nodding the head and shaking the head for disapproval. But in some countries, the opposite gestures may be used, or other gestures (via hand and arm movements) may be signals for approval. Thus, if you should be asked to negotiate with a foreigner, you should study cultural differences, including the meaning of embracing, handshakes (tight vs. loose), hand signals, eye contact, and body movements (crossing legs). Even exchanging business cards with the correct hand is indicative of one's culture.

One of the most telling signs of a good communicator is the quality of the voice and command of language. A soft tone (but not monotone) with crisp enunciation of words enhances your presentation. Good diction, proper grammar, and an intelligent use of language with a colorful and varied vocabulary are essential. You should never raise your voice, especially if you have lost your temper.

Selecting Your Team Members

In negotiations, the company's negotiator is its spokesperson. As such, he or she has certain traits that make him or her unique, including:

- A combination of motivation, skill, power, and self-confidence

- The ability to plan

- High integrity and ethical behavior

- The ability to think clearly under stressful conditions

■ Good judgment

■ Being a good listener and communicator

■ Personal regard for members of the team and empathy for the opponent

Selecting a negotiating team depends on the scope of the program—its technical requirements, its complexity, details in pricing, cost breakdown, and delivery schedules. The team consists of a group of specialists who help establish negotiating strategies and review and evaluate a proposal. The negotiator is the key person on the team. He or she may be assisted by the following experts (refer to Figure 2):

■ A *price/cost analyst* to assist in making recommendations on pricing matters

■ *Engineering or other technical personnel* whose responsibilities may include determining technical requirements, preparing independent cost estimates, and developing technical evaluation criteria for evaluation of the proposal

■ *Other specialists* in such areas as production, quality assurance, and manufacturing practices or techniques (selected according to your need for expert recommendations and general "know-how")

■ A member of the *legal department* to identify any contract inadequacies or inconsistencies before they become problems, and to review contract terms and conditions

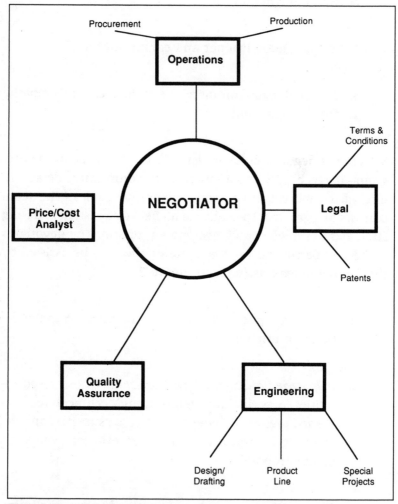

Figure 2: A Typical Negotiating Team

Writing the Memorandum of Agreement

A memorandum of agreement (Figure 3) is usually written by the buyer and reviewed by the seller upon completion of negotiations, to summarize the results of a negotiation. It should be signed by the negotiators for both parties. At a minimum,

MEMORANDUM OF AGREEMENT

The following summarizes an agreement between the Seller,
The Widget Company, and the Buyer, XYZ Manufacturing
Company, for the procurement of Widgets and for providing
Maintenance Service. The date of the agreement is 20
December 1991 and shall remain valid until 20 March 1992.
(Note: In the event an order is not issued prior to this
later date, the Buyer and Seller shall agree in writing to
either terminate or extend this agreement.)

Work Content and Schedules
The Widget Company shall supply one-hundred and fifty (150)
widgets at a rate of fifteen (15) per month, starting nine
(9) months after receipt of order, and shall provide in-
field service for the first three (3) units at XYZ's
facility in Anaheim, California, for a duration of six (6)
months, per statement of work XYZ-10001.

Prices
The initial three (3) units, including service, is priced
at $30,000 total fixed price; the remaining units are
priced at $1,250 each, fixed price. Total price = $213,750.

Terms and Conditions
All terms and conditions shall be in accordance to XYZ T/C
document no. XYZ-TC-101.

Miscellany
All special tools and fixtures shall be supplied by The
Widget Company at no extra charge.

Agreed to:

_____   _____   _____   _____

I.M.Seller   Date   I.M.Buyer   Date

Figure 3: A Sample Memorandum of Agreement

it should contain the defined work content/requirements,
schedules, final price(s), and terms and conditions. It should
be dated to indicate the length of time the agreement will be
honored or remain valid. Additional items that may be also
included in the memorandum include: options for deferred

work tasks, special incentive clauses that may be profit-oriented, and special tools and test equipment that may be supplied by the buyer. An agreement that is well written may be readily converted into a contract or purchase order.

Terms and Conditions

The renowned movie mogul Samuel B. Goldwyn once said: "A verbal agreement is not worth the paper it's written on!" Be leery of verbal agreements—get it in writing, especially the terms and conditions (T&C) of an agreement. The negotiator must be familiar with T&C because legal responsibilities also fall on the negotiator's shoulders.

Generally, T&C are based on two types of regulations: (1) government regulations that follow Federal Acquisition Regulation (FAR) clauses, and (2) the Uniform Commercial Code (UCC) for other than government-regulated programs. Both types of regulations cover items such as the terms and conditions for acceptance of an order, packaging and shipping, taxes and duties, warranty, inspection, default, changes or modifications, tools and materials, patents, termination, indemnity, and waivers.

In commercial (i.e., non-governmental) practice, the Uniform Commercial Code was enacted to regulate normal business practices and generally does not regulate or enforce conducting company operations and managing a company in any particular way. Thus, courts and parties to contracts liberally construe the principles of the UCC in normal business transactions. The parties can agree to anything so long as their agreement is provided by contract, shows good faith and reasonableness, and does not conflict with civil and criminal statutes. The principles of the UCC become applicable when:

- A provision is inadvertently omitted from a contract. (UCC may provide that "missing link")

- There are inconsistencies in some of the contract provisions. (UCC may help resolve them)

- As a minimum, the contract contains the identification of the parties, the subject matter, quantity and price.

The UCC follows English law and is recognized in all states, the District of Columbia, and Virgin Islands except Louisiana, whose legal traditions are derived from the laws of France. Individual state court decisions may follow their own interpretation of the UCC. However, interpretations by supreme courts of heavily industrialized states (California, Illinois, Michigan, New Jersey, New York, Ohio, Pennsylvania, and Texas) are often followed by courts in other states.

The UCC applies only to the purchase and sale of goods or merchandise. Furthermore, the UCC applies only to the purchase and sale of goods between merchants, and not between individuals (or consumers) and merchants. It is not applicable to real estate contracts, service contracts, consulting agreements, or repair agreements. Also, it does not apply to leasing equipment or software license and nondisclosure agreements.

The Federal Acquisition Regulations, which cover government contracts, are separated into 53 parts. FAR Part 52, containing several hundred clauses, is most prominent and applicable to both prime contractors and subcontractors.

CHAPTER 10

Sizing Up the Opposition

Your effectiveness as a negotiator depends on developing your own skills and effectively using the team concept. To be really successful at negotiations, you must also size up your opponent and his or her firepower. For example, does he or she have the capability and competency to supply products or services that you require? Does the opponent's company have a staff of adequate personnel to demonstrate satisfactory performance? Will the price you agree to be fair and reasonable? This chapter addresses two major areas to consider prior to scheduling negotiation sessions and, especially, before making that deal: (1) reviewing the other company's ability to meet your needs, and (2) evaluating a proposal prior to negotiation.

Getting to Know the Opponent's Company

In trying to determine if your opponent's company can provide the quality product under negotiation, and whether it can deliver it on schedule, several factors or characteristics of the other company should be considered. The factors below are not listed in order of importance since they should be considered equally when selecting a company for adequacy of performance.

Ethical Behavior

As a negotiator, you should try to deal with companies that display high ethical standards. It is crucial that a company is not engaged in any litigation involving misconduct that may prevent it from fully complying with any deal that is completed. This requirement is more relevant to government-oriented programs. A review of a company's commitment to business ethics and individual ethical behavior may help. (For example, refer to Appendix A for one company's adopted principles.)

Financial Capability

Are the other company's financial resources adequate to assure successful completion of the program to which you and your opponent have agreed? Are resources available to meet program needs for required facilities and equipment, material and personnel? Have you checked if the company is included in *Fortune* or *Standard & Poor's* "500 list"? If not, perhaps you should obtain a Dun & Bradstreet financial report, from which a comparison between cash assets and cash liabilities can be made and the company's performance in making payments of invoices reviewed. Your own company's accountant or accounting department can help you review and rate the other company's financial status.

Production Capability

The company's ability to plan, control, and integrate its human resources and facilities should be reviewed, including checking the system used by its management to control schedules and to assure timely deliveries. (Has the system been computerized?) The company's past performance on other programs and work performed for your company should be reviewed to determine degrees of satisfaction. Assistance from your manufacturing department can be helpful to review unfamiliar details.

Quality Assurance

Recently, Total Quality Management (TQM) has been a topic that companies have begun to consider in improving products and services, especially in light of tougher worldwide competition. Therefore, you should compare your requirements for quality to determine the adequacy of the company's quality assurance system and organization. Here again, you will most likely require assistance from your experts with quality assurance expertise.

Technical Capability

Does the company have the necessary experience and knowledge for meeting the specified technical requirements? During negotiation, your team must be convinced that the company can perform and satisfy the program needs. As it often happens, the wrong company can get the work for the right price. You should consider the company's experience for the same and similar applications and whether the company has retained its technical capability to produce or perform services despite past staff reductions or interruptions that have interfered with continuous production.

Evaluating Your Opponent's Proposal

In sizing up your opponent, knowledge of the responsibilities of both the seller and buyer that are associated with program proposal efforts is essential. A buyer has the responsibility of establishing program requirements and soliciting bids (proposals) from qualified sources of supply (the sellers). The buyer will evaluate proposals to assure they meet the program requirements. Selection of a qualified seller will depend on completing negotiations satisfactorily and familiarity of your opponent's company (as covered by the previous section).

The seller follows the guidelines of the buyer's request for a proposal and is prepared to negotiate the proposal. For some programs (or contracts), acceptance of the lowest bidder (seller) negates the necessity to negotiate. But in this age of high technology and specialization, where complexity of products and services require a buyer to better understand what is being procured, negotiations are almost mandatory.

Thus, a successful compromise between both parties in a negotiation is challenging. A buyer must be able to evaluate the potential effectiveness of a seller's proposal. This often requires having an adequate technical staff—engineers and supporting technicians—to assist in the preparations for negotiations. However, before proceeding with negotiations, the buyer should follow procedures to assure that the seller potentially has the capability, capacity, and qualifications to perform the specified workscope and satisfactorily meet schedules. And, most importantly, the buyer must be convinced that the seller's prices are reasonably within cost or pricing constraints.

To perform a thorough review, plan to consider key elements of a proposal. If the size of the program warrants it, a risk appraisal also may be performed to forecast the outcome or relative success of a program. These activities assist in rating the acceptability of the proposal.

Depending on the complexity or dollar value of a buy, a proposal may include the following main selections:

1. A *technical description* of the planned workscope

2. The *cost estimates*, perhaps segregated by work task levels or cost elements that account for primary and supportive tasks in consideration of those descriptions contained in the other sections

3. *Schedules* that demonstrate how the contractor plans to meet required end item delivery dates for both hardware and documentation

4. A treatise about *management* of the proposed program, which, as a minimum, may include a description of the organization to be employed, the key personnel, cost/schedule control, and reporting techniques

In reviewing a proposal, a buyer's review team may be required to consider:

1. Aspects of design approaches that fit the technical requirements

2. Cost by work task breakdown

3. Schedules, separated by an in-depth review of the seller's plans

4. The aspects of management within each of the key elements and within a "risk appraisal" that assigns risk levels (low to high) to cost, schedule, and technical aspects of the proposal

The proposal should be reviewed initially to identify any additional information or clarifications that may be needed. Prior to negotiations, a fact-finding conference may be held with the seller to obtain answers and, if necessary, to discuss the submittal of revisions to the proposal for incorporation of amendments that may result from the meeting. Based on the proposal and its modifications being deemed complete, negotiations may then begin. When an agreement is reached, it should be summarized in a memorandum of agreement (refer to Chapter 9).

CHAPTER **11**

The Personality Game: The Negotiator as Detective

In general it is recognized that people have different personality traits, different motives, and different needs. Negotiators are tasked with observing the personality traits of other key players in addition to observing behavior patterns and body language as discussed in Chapter 9. Practical experience helps in understanding various personality types and how to cope with and comfortably relate to them. The strategies and tactics of negotiations can thus be adapted to whomever is your counterpart. Therefore, be cautious; at the beginning of each negotiation, study the person with whom you will be dealing. The list below describes generally recognizable personalities (but are not, of course, completely comprehensive):

■ The *decisive* person is quick to make decisions.

■ The *deliberate* person may react slowly and will not be satisfied until he gets all the facts.

■ The *sociable* person is friendly and does not like to say no; you need to use stronger tactics than usual to get him or her to reach an agreement.

■ The *skeptical* person is a doubting Thomas who must be led into the decision until convinced it is to his or her advantage.

■ The *impulsive* person vacillates in decision making, first agreeing, then disagreeing. You must catch this person in a positive swing to close a deal.

■ The *submissive* person wants to be told what to do. Deals usually can be completed quickly.

Whom You May Encounter at Negotiations

In addition to recognizing general personality traits, recognition of specific personality types that are encountered at negotiations is useful in anticipating an opponent's behavior. Four recognizable basic personalities are:

1. The *ambitious* person focuses more on achieving results than dealing effectively with people. Ambitious people sometimes appear uncommunicative but are stable, independent, and competitive in relationships with others. While usually projecting a pleasant and extremely charming personality, they may, in an ef-

fort to succeed, mistreat others. They rarely recognize or reward individuals for meritorious performance or service.

2. An *extrovert* tends to be communicative, warm, and approachable, yet is also competitive. Extroverts seem to want you as a friend but in reality only want you to follow and support their ambitions. Relationships with extroverts during negotiations are usually short-lived and end when their goals are reached.

3. The *friend* is the most people-oriented of the four basic personality styles. Friends recognize people as individuals rather than using them to achieve results or political influence. Friends look for and get supportive opinions. They display friendliness but avoid taking risks.

4. The *introvert* is generally uncommunicative, level-headed, and independent. Introverts may appear cooperative but are cautious in acting friendly (thinking it may cost something in return) and are primarily concerned with closing a deal without much interaction with you and, especially, without any personal involvement.

Troubleshooting: Coping with Difficult Opponents

Dealing with difficult opposing negotiators involves understanding what makes them tick. Knowing the proper strategies or tactics helps the negotiation proceed more efficiently, with maximum cooperation and minimal conflict. Examples of difficult negotiators are:

1. *Hostile*: This negotiator is the wise-cracker whose cutting remarks put you on the defensive. Hostile negotiators can be supercritical and may bully you; they will often find a way to intimidate you.

2. *Explosive*: This negotiator has a short fuse and is short-tempered. Explosive negotiators create highly manipulative and emotional confrontations in order to dissuade lengthy negotiations, often forcing an opponent to make rash decisions. Watch out: Their behavior may also be a ploy to embarrass you in front of others.

3. *Know-It-All*: This negotiator calls himself or herself an expert. But when know-it-alls are wrong, they swiftly pass the buck and blame someone else for any problems.

4. *Pessimist*: This negotiator will delay decisions until it is too late to reach them. Pessimists remain negative and inflexible, which makes it difficult to reach agreements.

5. *Faker*: You rarely know where you stand with this negotiator. Fakers always seem to agree, but secretly don't and often forget earlier agreements that you thought were understood and confirmed.

6. *Indecisive*: This negotiator avoids controversy and may never let you know where he or she stands. He or she often poses nit-picking objections to even the most lucid and acceptable proposals.

7. *Con Artist*: This type can look you straight in the eyes and be deceptive. Con artists are willing to lie to win points for their companies.

Now that you are able to recognize difficult negotiators, what can you do about them? Even though you cannot change them, you can often anticipate their particular traits and turn the negotiations to your advantage.

Here are some hints on softening aggressive attitudes when dealing with difficult negotiators. First, pay attention to what is being said and *how* it's being said. Listen to the tone and volume of the voice (for example, constantly raising one's voice often indicates an aggressive personality type). If perhaps your questions have not been answered, be more patient, tolerant, and flexible by rephrasing questions or responses. If the other person shouts, react by speaking in a more even, calm tone. The other person may then react by lowering his or her voice.

When speaking, speed up or slow down your tempo to pace the negotiations. Watch your volume. Ask questions that lead to your objectives. You must communicate clearly so that you are fully understood.

Trust and cooperation are essential for both sides to work together. Always attempt to build trust and cooperation with a difficult person (after all, you have no choice but to work with that individual). Explain that reaching an agreement is of mutual interest. Don't get frustrated if the difficult negotiator fails to recognize advantages, disadvantages, and explanations of changes to a negotiated item. Respond to the other person's gestures and body language to maintain a trusting relationship without making the other person feel that you are mimicking his or her behavior. Nodding your head for a positive response (a suggestive power) is a good way to get the other person, subconsciously, to agree.

Recognize other negotiator's differences, styles, priorities, and temperaments. Be more assertive, yet less aggressive or passive in your behavior. Aggressive behavior appears to represent power but often reveals insecurity and upsets the people around you. Passive people think that you are right and they are wrong, while aggressive individuals believe they are right and you are not. But assertive people are willing to work out an agreement, recognizing that no one is perfect. They recognize that people must get along to close deals that satisfy everyone.

Try asking questions rather than making assertions or assumptions. Find out if your team agrees with the other side's statements or criticism. Even if *you* feel ready to close a deal before you have consulted with your team, don't openly admit it until you have checked with the team for feedback. But if you have questions or concerns, ask the other side for more specific information. Get them to define the problem fully before trying to reconcile differences.

In addition, you must recognize the types of difficult personalities who may be members of your team and deal with them accordingly. If a team member gets out of hand, you should caucus and speak to the individual before reconvening, to prevent either you or the team member from displaying behavior that may prevent or delay an agreement. As the team leader, you may avoid embarrassment or conflict by requesting that the individual save comments until there is an appropriate time to offer them. If necessary, advise the person to take a break from the meeting to collect his or her thoughts or to tone down any inflammatory comments.

Remember to give each person the benefit of the doubt; he or she may not be intentionally destroying the negotiations. Let the person save face, especially if he or she realizes that you recognize the emotional behavior pattern. If treated fairly, your team member will most likely become receptive to exchanging information and reaching agreement instead of becoming progressively more difficult to handle. With limited time to reach agreement, it is crucial that negotiations run smoothly and efficiently. But do not rush the negotiations; give the other side the courtesy of listening to its presentation and rebuttals. By being discourteous, you may give the impression that you are not concerned about what it may have to offer, which may lead to an unsatisfactory agreement or a breakdown in communication.

CHAPTER 12

Negotiation and Sales

No book about negotiations should neglect the most established and experienced group of negotiators of history: salespersons. The salesperson must be an outstanding negotiator, dealing with people with a calm yet enthusiastic manner, effectively marketing products or services by filling or creating needs. Many sales professionals are also business negotiators. Both specialties require diplomacy as well as business policies to please both clients and their managers. This chapter describes the salesperson as a negotiator and discusses the similarity of closing sales (the salesperson's technique) to negotiating.

A salesperson is one who:

- Prospects for leads or sells on recall or referral basis

- Makes convincing presentations

- Applies closing techniques to complete sales

An experienced, well-qualified salesperson has learned to prepare and present a sales pitch that has maximum impact. Some companies provide pre-scripted sales presentations, while others allow their sales personnel to create their own presentations. In either case, the salesperson must be capable of arousing interest in and stimulating desire for products. As a motivator, he or she has learned to close sales. But before closing deals, the salesperson must learn how to be effective without irritating the prospective customer and how to leave the client with a positive impression of the salesperson (and of the product) so that the door is left open for future sales.

The Salesperson as Negotiator

A salesperson should be authorized to act on behalf of a firm for the price and condition of sale. The salesperson and his or her company must recognize that a buyer's interest may change from doing business as usual with one company to buying on a competitive basis. Thus, salespersons who formerly may have had a "take it or leave it" attitude now learn to be flexible. They must concentrate on satisfying a customer instead of just selling a product.

As a negotiator, the salesperson reacts to a customer's needs, shows the buyer the benefits of the product or services, and attempts to demonstrate the benefits by applying both sales and post-selling techniques to assure that the customer does not renege on the agreement to buy.

Sales negotiations, like any other business negotiations, require preparation prior to holding any sessions with a buyer. For example, preparation may include, besides becoming knowledgeable about the product, planning for sales presentations that may include:

- Introducing the firm you represent—its experience, reliability, reputation, and capability
  To illustrate: "My company, XYZ Widgets, has been producing widgets for the past ten years and is included in the Fortune 500. Users of our product include many well-known industrial firms all of whom can attest to its reliable and dependable performance."

- Researching information about the buyer and the buyer's company, including products or services that may be needed

- Identifying possible competitors and competitive products, if relevant

- Thinking about how you might assist or benefit the buyer by providing continual supportive service after agreement, including written warranties and lists of local repair centers

- Establishing a range of acceptable price offers

A salesperson is responsible, above all, for getting orders, but first must be thoroughly familiar with the features of the product or services to be sold and be convinced that he or she represents a reputable firm. The salesperson must be armed with reasons (e.g. better delivery schedules or warranties) why a customer should buy from his or her firm and not from competitors. If the salesperson is not prepared to counteract claims made by a qualified competitor or to offer lower prices, then he or she might as well end the sales presentation or negotiation right then before being tempted, out of desperation, to exaggerate claims about the product or services to complete that sale.

To illustrate: (A False Claim): You haven't made a sale all day; the last client likes your product but not your price. You claim that your product will last 50 percent longer (an unfounded claim) and is well worth that 20 percent higher price than your competitor's price.

Sales strategies and tactics are similar to those developed for other business negotiations and are often considered closing techniques for reaching agreements.

The Similarities of Negotiating and Closing

Negotiating techniques and the closing techniques used in sales are closely related. Both techniques result in either acceptance or rejection. When a sales presentation is rejected, it may mean that the buyer was not convinced to buy; whereas in negotiating, proposals may be rejected until a compromise agreement is reached. The difference lies primarily with product (or service) needs of the buyer and if he or she is doing the soliciting. Negotiating, however, may encompass both closing and negotiating techniques simultaneously; the buyer may only agree to buy when convinced the price is reasonable.

To illustrate: You are negotiating a contract, and the buyer is not convinced that your price is right. You ask if the price were reduced by ten percent, would the buyer still agree? And he does!

The primary difference between closing and negotiating is that closing is a technique primarily used by the seller, while negotiating is used by both the seller and the buyer.

The similarities between closing and negotiating are most apparent when dealing with difficult customers and deadlocks. The tactics used to break negotiation deadlocks may very well apply to closing.

In closing, as in negotiating, it is important to project a positive attitude; one should be persistent but remain calm, composed, and ready for the least expected comment or query. A salesperson must be prepared to respond to questions relating to price, packaging, or the goal of reaching agreement and, of course, the *sale*.

Closing also requires knowing what technique to apply. Expertise in closing is primarily developed through experience. Experience will also help you better understand body language to overcome objections. You will discover which techniques best suit your personality and your particular client. To a degree, you are an actor; cordial and restrained with an aggressive client, but firm and dynamic with a less decisive client. You must be aware of a variety of strategies and tactics for your own use and also to understand those the buyer may use. Your closing approach must reflect your confidence that the final terms of any agreement will be satisfactory to both you and the buyer; that your offer represents a compromise.

Remember, in handling objections you should never argue back. You can simply reiterate your points and offer a better explanation. The temptation to reply in a hostile way is always present.

To illustrate: You, as a salesperson, are challenged by a person who is balking at buying your product and who says, "I think you're wasting my time . . . trying to sell this widget to me . . ." If you respond in a rude and indignant manner, you will almost certainly lose the sale. You may win the argument, but reaching an agreement will be unlikely. (Refer to Chapter 7 for What Went Wrong.)

In handling objections, turn them into reasons for acceptance; emphasize the positive and your willingness to handle *any* concerns the buyer may have. Price consideration, delivery, terms and conditions, and so on can be worked out when both sides have the desire to agree. Try to anticipate the other side's arguments, and come to negotiations readily equipped with the answers.

Key issues to remember that lead to success as a salesperson are highlighted below:

Failure to agree may be due to:

- Failure to adequately demonstrate the product (or services)

- A poor mental attitude

- Offending the opponent: appearing hostile or unnecessarily argumentative

To overcome these failures, remember to:

- Listen carefully to the opponent

- Answer any objections, completely and in detail

- Turn objections around so that they become reasons to accept your arguments
  To illustrate: "If this widget is guaranteed for two years rather than one year, then you would buy it, correct?"

- Improve the impression you make (e.g., mannerisms, speech)

Preparations for winning agreements include:

- A pleasant and neatly dressed appearance

- Listening attentively and being alert and responsive (which communicates that you acknowledge your opponent's needs)

- Strong, convincing, and enthusiastic presentations

- Enthusiasm

- Answering objections willingly and concisely

- Expressing confidence but *not* arrogance or aggressiveness

- Ending with a win-win agreement that satisfies both sides

To summarize closing techniques, they may include:

- Finding out what is wanted and needed before convincing the buyer to buy

- Overcoming the other party's fear of not getting the best deal for the price, of overpaying, or of buying something that is not needed

- Explaining and dismissing objections before they arise

- Convincing the other party (without being intimidating) that dealing with you is preferable to dealing with someone else

- Never appearing to argue (agree by using the "Yes, but" technique)

APPENDIX A

A Negotiator's Guide to Ethics and Conduct

It is inherent in negotiations that the negotiator is seen—willingly or not—as the representative of a company's corporate culture. Since the negotiator's actions and conduct will be interpreted as reflecting the company, it is important that he or she remain within the bounds of business ethics.

Many companies have already adopted a set of principles of business ethics and conduct that acknowledge and address corporate responsibilities. While these principles may vary according to the needs of individual companies (a retail business or bank may have different employee standards than those of a nonprofit government agency) there is a basic code of ethics accepted by the industry. The Unisys Corporation offers an excellent example in their 1988 pamphlet, *Handbook of Ethical Business Practices*, which is adapted below.

Corporate Ethics and Conduct

Written Code of Business Ethics and Conduct

A company's code of business ethics and conduct should embody the values that it and its employees hold most important. For a negotiator, the code represents the commitment of the company and its employees to work for its customers, shareholders, and the nation. It is important, therefore, that a negotiator's written code explicitly address that commitment, including a statement of the standards of conduct for all employees in their relationships to the company as well as in their dealings with customers, suppliers, and consultants.

Employees' Ethical Responsibilities

A company's code of business ethics and conduct should embody the basic values of the company and should become a way of life—an honor system—for every employee. A code is more than mere words or abstract ideals. Each employee is responsible for adhering to the code—as representatives of the company, and also in terms of interacting with colleagues. Failure to report infractions can erode trust among employees. Communication and training are critical in preparing employees to meet ethical responsibilities.

Corporate Responsibility to Employees

Every company must ensure that employees have the opportunity to fulfill their responsibilities to preserve the integrity of the honor system. Employees should be free to report suspected violations of the code to the company without fear of retribution by having a confidential reporting channel readily available. It is critical that companies create and maintain an environment of openness where disclosures are both accepted and expected. Employees must believe that reporting misconduct is in the best interest of the company and that they are not risking their jobs by pointing out violations. This removes any legitimate rationale for employees to delay reporting alleged violations or for former employees to allege past offenses by former employers or associates. To receive and investigate employee allegations of violations of the corporate code of business ethics and conduct, negotiators may use a review board, a corporate ethics or compliance office or other similar objective organization.

Corporate Responsibility to the Government

It is the responsibility of each company to aggressively self-govern. Companies may establish procedures for voluntarily reporting to appropriate government authorities violations of federal laws. In the past, much importance has been placed on whether internal company monitoring has uncovered deficiencies *before* discovery by governmental audit. Corporate and government audit and control mechanisms should be used to identify and correct problems. Government and industry share this responsibility and must work together cooperatively and constructively to ensure compliance with federal procurement laws and to clarify any ambiguities that may exist.

Public Accountability

Public accountability may require each company to employ independent public accountants, or similar independent organizations, to periodically complete and submit replies to questionnaires to an external independent research company that will report the results for the industry as a whole and release the data to both the companies and publicly.

Individual Ethical Behavior
(Dealing Honestly with Customers, Suppliers, and Consultants)
Contract Negotiation

In negotiating contracts, you should be accurate and complete in all representations. Submitting a proposal, quotation, or other document or statement to the government that is false, incomplete, or misleading can result in civil and/or criminal liability for the company, the involved employees, and supervisors. In negotiating contracts with the government, one is obligated to disclose current, accurate, and complete cost and pricing data.

Product Quality

A firm should be committed to delivering quality products that meet quality standards and should not deliver products that are made from inferior materials, are not properly tested, or otherwise fail to meet contract specifications.

Competitive Analysis

In conducting market analysis, avoid the acceptance or use of information that may be considered proprietary by your competitors.

Charging of Costs/Timecard Reporting

Employees who file timecards must be particularly careful to do so in a complete, accurate, and timely manner to ensure that hours worked and incurred costs are applied to the proper cost account or program. No cost may be charged or allocated to a government contract if the cost is unallowable by regulation or by contract or program provisions.

The employee's signature on a timecard is a representation that the timecard accurately reflects the number of hours worked on the specified project or work order. The supervisor's signature is a representation that the timecard has been reviewed and that steps have been taken to verify the validity of the hours reported and the correctness of the allocation of the hours.

Hiring of Federal Employees

Complex rules govern the recruitment and employment of government employees in private industry. A company's human resources department must provide necessary clearance to discuss possible employment with, make offers to, or hire (as an employee or consultant) any current or former government employee.

Use Company Resources Properly
Making Political Contributions

Do not contribute or donate company funds, products, services, or other resources for any political cause, party, or candidate. (You may make voluntary *personal* contributions to a political action committee or to any lawful political cause, party, or candidate so long as you do not represent that such contributions come from the corporation.)

Providing Courtesies to Customers or Suppliers

Employees should never offer any type of business courtesies to a customer for purposes of obtaining favorable treatment or advantages. To avoid the appearance of any impropriety, do not provide a customer or supplier with gifts or promotional items of more than nominal value. Except for government customers or representatives, you may pay for a reasonably priced meal, refreshment, and/or entertainment expenses for customers and suppliers associated with a *business* meeting.

For U.S. Government Customers

Employees should not provide or pay for any meal, refreshment or entertainment, travel, and lodging expenses of any government employee without the advance written approval of the company's legal department.

Dealing with Foreign Officials

Do not promise, offer, or make any payments in money, products, or services to any foreign official in exchange for or in

order to induce favorable business treatment or to affect any
government decision. In some foreign countries, the law may
permit minor payments to clerical personnel to expedite performance of their duties. Such minor payments may be made
only with the express approval of the country's general manager on advice of the law department, but must never exceed
$50 per payment and must never be made to gain or retain
business.

Accurate Books and Accounts

All payments and other transactions must be properly authorized by management and be accurately and completely
recorded on the company's books and records in accordance
with generally accepted accounting principles and established
corporate accounting policies. Make no false, incomplete, or
misleading entries. No undisclosed or unrecorded corporate
funds should be established for any purpose, nor should company funds be placed in any personal or noncorporate account.
All corporate assets must be properly protected and asset records regularly compared with actual assets; any variances
should be reconciled.

Do Not Abuse Your Position

A company expects you to devote your full working time and
efforts to a company's interests and to avoid any activity that
might detract from or conflict with a company's interests. In
particular:

Conflict of Interest

Remember to avoid employment as a consultant or other business relationship, with a competitor, customer, or supplier of
the firm nor invest in any competitor, customer, or supplier.
Outside employment may also constitute a conflict of interest
if it places an employee in the position of appearing to rep-

resent the company and involves providing goods or services substantially similar to those provided by the company.

Insider Trading

Do not trade in the securities of any company, or buy or sell any property or assets, on the basis of nonpublic information that was acquired through one's employment, whether such information may come from your company or from another company.

Acceptance of Business Courtesies

Never accept anything of value from someone doing business with you where a gratuity is offered in exchange for any type of favorable treatment! Do not accept any gifts or promotional items of more than nominal value. You may accept meals, drinks, or entertainment, but only if such courtesies are unsolicited and reasonable in amount. Such courtesies must also be directly connected with business discussion, unless your supervisor approves an exception. Do not accept free lodging or reimbursement for travel expenses from anyone outside your company.

Company Restricted Information

Do not disclose to any outside party, except as specifically authorized by management, any nonpublic business, financial, personnel, or technological information, plans, or data that were acquired during employment. Upon termination of employment, do not copy, take, or retain any documents containing restricted information. The prohibition against disclosing restricted information extends beyond your period of employment. (Your agreement to protect the confidentiality of such information in perpetuity is considered an important condition of employment.)

Government Classified and Proprietary Information

Employees with valid security clearances who have access to classified information must ensure that such information is handled in accordance with federal regulations and procedures. These restrictions apply to any form of information, whether written or in electronic form. A company should not solicit nor receive any sensitive proprietary internal government information, including budgetary or program information, before it is available through normal processes.

Reporting Violations and Disciplinary Actions

Strict adherence to codes of ethical conduct is vital. Supervisors may be held responsible for ensuring that employees adhere to the provisions of any code. To provide clarification or guidance on any point in the code, a human resources department may be given organizational responsibility.

Employees are expected to report any suspected violations of the code or other irregularities to their supervisor, or a company designated ombudsman. No retribution of any kind should be taken against an employee due to reporting any suspected violation of the code or any irregularity. The report should be treated confidentially, consistent with fair and rigorous enforcement of the code. Violations of the code may result in disciplinary action ranging from warnings and reprimand to discharge or even the filing of a civil or criminal complaint.

APPENDIX B

Suggested Further Reading

Beier, Ernst G. and Valens, Evans G., *People-Reading*, Warner Books, New York, 1975.

Berne, Eric, *Games People Play*, Grove Press, New York, 1964.

Cohen, Herb, *You Can Negotiate Anything*, Bantam Books, New York, 1980.

Crosby, Philip B., *The Art of Getting Your Own Sweet Way*, McGraw-Hill, New York, 1981.

Fisher, Roger and Brown, Scott, *Getting Together*, Penguin Books, New York, 1988.

Fisher, Roger and Ury, William, *Getting to Yes*, Penguin Books, New York, 1981.

Girard, Joe, *How to Sell Anything to Anybody*, Warner Books, New York, 1977.

Harris, Charles E., *Business Negotiating Power*, Van Nostrand Reinhold Co., New York, 1983.

Hartman, George M., *How to Negotiate a Bigger Raise*, Barron's, New York, 1991.

Hinde, Robert A., *Non-Verbal Communication*, Cambridge University Press, London, 1972.

Jandt, Fred E., *Win-Win Negotiating*, John Wiley & Sons, New York, 1985.

Karrass, Chester L., *Give and Take*, Thomas Y. Crowell, New York, 1974.

———. *The Negotiating Game*, Thomas Y. Crowell, New York, 1970.

Kelly, Paul J., *Situation Selling*, American Management Association, New York, 1988.

Korda, Michael, *Power How to Get It, How to Use It*, Random House, New York, 1975.

McCormack, Mark H., *What They Didn't Teach You at Harvard Business School*, Bantam Books, New York, 1984.

National Contract Management Association, *Advanced Negotiations*, Workshop Participation Guide, Vienna, Va., 1990.

———. *Negotiation Procedures and Strategies Training Manual*, Vienna, Va., 1983.

Nierenberg, Gerard I., *The Art of Negotiating*, Pocket Books, New York, 1981.

———. *Creative Business Negotiating*, Hawthorne Books, New York, 1971.

Nierenberg, Gerard I. and Calero, Henry H., *How to Read a Person Like a Book*, Pocket Books, New York, 1971.

———. *Meta-Talk*, Cornerstone, New York, 1980.

Pease, Allan, *Signals: How to Use Body Language for Power, Success and Love*, Bantam Books, New York, 1981.

Poslums, Ronald J., *Negotiate Your Way to Financial Success*, G. P. Putnam's Sons, New York, 1987.

Raiffa, Howard, *The Art and Science of Negotiation*, Harvard University Press, Cambridge, Mass., 1982.

Reck, Ross R. and Long, Brian G., *The Win-Win Negotiator*, Pocket Books, New York, 1987.

Schatzki, Michael and Coffey, Wayne R., *Negotiation: The Art of Getting What You Want*, Signet Books, New York, 1981.

Sperber, Philip, *Fail-Safe Business Negotiating*, Prentice-Hall, Englewood Cliffs, N.J., 1983.

Torquato, John, *Why Winners Win*, American Management Association, New York, 1983.

Warschaw, Tessa A., *Winning by Negotiation*, McGraw-Hill, New York, 1980.